THIS BOOK
Belongs To:

_____

_____

_____

SOME IDEAS FOR THINGS YOU CAN DO WITH YOUR GIRLFRIEND ON VALENTINE'S DAY:

Romantic Dinner: Plan a romantic dinner at a nice restaurant or cook a special meal together at home. Set the mood with candles, soft music, and a beautifully set table.

Outdoor Adventure: If you both enjoy the outdoors, consider a day of hiking, biking, or a picnic in a scenic park. You can also plan a weekend getaway to a romantic destination.

Movie Night: Have a cozy movie night at home with your favorite films or romantic classics. Don't forget the popcorn and blankets!

DIY Spa Day: Create a spa experience at home with relaxing massages, face masks, and a bubble bath. Make it even more special with scented candles and soothing music.

Artistic Endeavors: Take a pottery or painting class together. Creating art can be a fun and romantic way to spend time together.

Stargazing: Find a quiet spot away from city lights, bring a blanket, and spend the evening stargazing. You can even download a stargazing app to help identify constellations.

———— ♥ ————

Wine Tasting: Visit a local winery or create your own wine tasting at home. Pair the wines with some delicious cheeses and chocolates.

Cooking Class: Take a cooking class together and learn how to make a new dish. It can be a fun and interactive way to bond while enjoying a delicious meal.

Scavenger Hunt: Plan a romantic scavenger hunt with clues leading to special places that hold meaning for your relationship.

Volunteer Together: Spend the day volunteering for a cause you both care about. It's a meaningful way to connect and make a positive impact.

Live Entertainment: Attend a concert, theater show, or comedy club for a night of entertainment.

Memory Lane: Take a trip down memory lane by revisiting the place where you first met or had your first date.
Share memories and reflect on your journey together.

——————— ♥ ———————

Copyright © 2024 All rights reserved.
No part of this book may be reproduced or transmitted in any form or by any means, electronic or mechanical, including photocopying, recording, or by any information storage and retrieval system, without permission in writing from the publisher.
This book is a work of fiction
. Names, characters, places, and incidents
either are products of the author's imagination
or are used fictitiously. Any resemblance to actual events or locales or persons, living or dead, is entirely coincidental.

COLOR TEST

MOVIE NIGHT

OUTDOOR ADVENTURE:

LIVE ENTERTAINMENT

MEMORY LANE

MARRY HER AND ABOVE ALL, LOVE HER

In love's gentle embrace, we find,
A dance of hearts, forever entwined.
Roses bloom and whispers say,
Happy Valentine's, my love, today.

www.ingramcontent.com/pod-product-compliance
Lightning Source LLC
Chambersburg PA
CBHW081121080526
44587CB00021B/3700